FRIENDSHIP
is like a
Seesaw

For Stuart, Riley and Charlie
— Shona Innes

For my ever best seesaw friend, Dorka
— Írisz Agócs

The Five Mile Press Pty Ltd
1 Centre Road, Scoresby
Victoria 3179 Australia
www.fivemile.com.au

Part of the Bonnier Publishing Group
www.bonnierpublishing.com

First published 2014

Printed in China 5 4 3 2 1

FRIENDSHIP
is like a
Seesaw

Shona Innes * Írisz Agócs

The Five Mile Press

Friendships are funny and precious things.
Friendships come in many shapes and sizes.

Friendships are built by the way
we get along with friends.

Friends can be old or new.
A good friendship is a very
special thing to have.

Good friends agree on the rules.

They do nice things for each other, they are kind and they help when we are feeling down.

Good friends takes turns, share and have fun together as they play.

Sometimes friendship can be
a little bit like a seesaw.
When friends play on a seesaw,
one side goes up,
the other side goes down.

And when one side goes down, the other side of the seesaw goes up.

When a seesaw is even on both sides, it is balanced.

Friendship is like a seesaw.
Sometimes you might feel up in the air
when your friend feels low.

Other times, you might feel down when your friend is up.

When a friendship is even on both
sides, it is balanced.

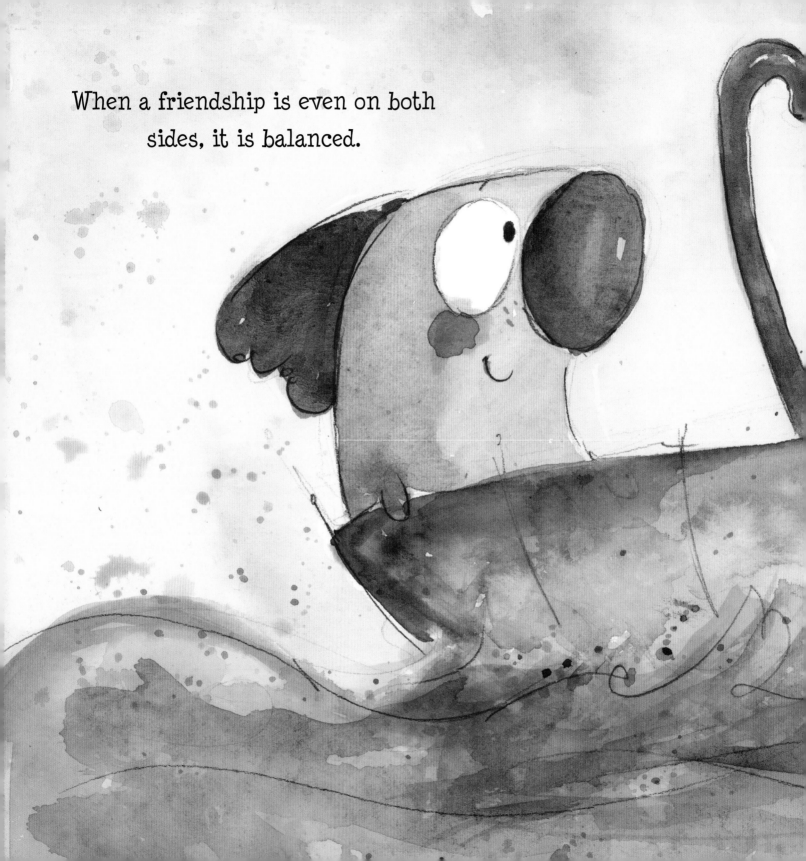

When things are balanced,
both friends feel happy.

Sometimes a friendship can get out of balance if one friend is feeling troubled or low.

It might be out of balance because
there is a problem that needs fixing.

A friendship can get out of balance if someone
is being bossy ...

Or if someone is being sooky.

Sometimes, instead of the friendship feeling good, we might feel bad about the friendship.

Friends might say or do hurtful things,
or leave us out of the fun.

When a friendship is uneven and troubled,
you might feel very sad or angry.

But there are things you can
do to re-balance and fix the friendship.

We can tell our friend that we are not happy and see if we can work it out together.

Sometimes we might need to stop and check
if our own friendship skills are working.

Sometimes, we might even need to take
a break from a friend for a while.

It can really hurt when a troubled friend
makes us feel bad. We might want to hurt
them back, but that will only make things worse.
Things will still be out of balance.

Instead, we can do lots of things that will make us feel better.

We can do nice things for other people, or play with other friends,

or enjoy some quiet time by ourself doing the things that we love to do.

One day we might decide to go back to the friendship.
Getting back the balance might take some time.

But when things are even again,
we can play and be happy together.

And maybe even laugh about
the troubles we had.

Friendship can be like that sometimes.